A STONE

UNTURNED

STEVE COOK

A Stone Unturned
Steve Cook

Published by ABeFree Publishing, 2022
ISBN 9781838440152
Copyright@SteveCook2022

Dedication and Appreciation
Thanks to ABeFree Publishing for formatting the soft-back edition.
http://www.buffry.org.uk/abefreepublishing.html
Cover photo by Jon Anderson

STEVE COOK

Steve Cook is a well-travelled son of a Norfolk farming family, a graduate from Norwich Arts School, a poet, artist, photographer, mechanic, farmer and inventor.

He has previously authored several books of poetry in the "Natural Allies" series and contributed to the following anthologies:

"Inside My Hat and Other Heads"

"Words of Weed and Wisdom"

4 ·XII· 01·

CONTENTS

DRACONIA

These measures of controlling pleasures
Vestiges of spirit empathy
Intertwine of sympathy
Beans with whirly windmills
Painted colours cobalt blue
Forming swirling freshly true
Scaring off pigeons
Into the woods a pace
All the reflections of another space
So off to woody grove
On a windy elbow rove
Constantly on the move
In a flock round at a pace
Forth in flight innocent grace over
In formation for metamorphosing a rock face
Quietly waving two or threes
Fours fives sixes join geese
Each returning straw or twig lime mixes

ASH-STRAY

The cat strode through twisted vines
The old past glass house of lime-wash beech
The sun-dial gives the times
And the boiler warms tomatoes and cress
All these herbs to help with stress
Sage, marjoram to brown rice stuffed green peppers
The shepherd in his shelter, rests his crook
Sits to boil coffee, an inhalation took.
Grampa's eggs and song book
A song thrush, shy and timid, came to rest
On top the hawthorn blossom high
He sung of bluebells in cool woodland glades
And of wood anemones soft
Of honey suckle evenings still and calm
In Maytime's twilight soft and scented
When lilac boughs are lost in purple haze
And rosebuds dream of summer
At night cherished nightingales eloquence heard
Can one sing more sweetly than that speckled
bird?
Our dreams down a quiet riverlet
Slow moving red glow
Dusk til dawn

18 LINES

The Dusty ol' Moon

One moment in your life.

Is fulfilment to uplift

Few moments pass

Then a feed for the survivor

The two thoughts rival

The telepathic link

Like our last wink

Or chortle

This is a pure river of water

Dripping trickling, rushing or dancing

The children splashing the Mothers washing

Clear cool effervescence

Lovers walk towards the wood, hands together

Wishing to find a path to guide their way

To wherever this may lead

As each other in their thoughts they need.

She bought freedom from another land

She came from another land

She brought freedom in her hand

A smile and wasn't that a bit funny

A cup of chai bye and bye

Sip by sip ashante

A SLEEP ON MOUSEHOLD

Soak up the aftermath

Resting 'twixt the chestnut

Upon the lower boughs

With artists all about on deck-chairs

White hats, white coats 'got to be a
circumstance

Where it doesn't matter whose to boast

Making cuppa's, hand out butter and toast

'Cause there's a stroll

'A lump of ol' coal

An emotional friend has a soul

At the bottom of the sea lives a flat soul

The tales to be told, are too cold?

You must have kindliness from someone to
borrow

Have a little nap

And shelter from life's sorrow.

You might be sitting

Pondering a new start

At standing up for a good life

An eco-climate village pond and a bevy of
ducks

A goose clapping out for attention

The next thought is just good intention

Well maybe we'll catch the papers tomorrow.

MISTY

Past the subterranean cattle mooing meadow

butter-cups along the rivulets dancing o'er the shallows

And the hemp oil follows; the black grass fallows,

Craft fair produce along the blickers road

Which has such beauty as demand easy code

On many a summertime romance blowed

The precedents of the charitable lady abode

The chestnuts and tall beech breaths flowed

On the misty dawns when the suns rays explode

Sunlight upon a vista so calm in its maintained upkeep

It's for people to amaze ….

With a plenitude of anachronistic beauty

Where man displayed his temperance to duty

Shown in the catchment of the cairn of the lakes.

So on a sunny summer day a Vincent Tavohub brakes

Well the Vat 69 flowed on scotch on the rocks

Bah! went the sheep, the oak field haystacks
heat

The lambs bleat to their mothers rolled over
defeat

Hundreds of gnarled years the branches
protested

A life of leisurely, yarns and tittle-tattle

Friends with their young grandfathers
connected

Bee-honey in mega conical hand-made pots

Wooster-tweed, baskets of reed, shallow basket
bottle cask

SHADE LOSS

Peace be unto the fan blowing
Waiting now is unity flowering
Gently laid bed of stupendous air
Flowing out over the flood-plain wi' good cheer
Of the cavernous bedrock waters trickling
Porously where the Penine rain shadow
Broke through with heavenly clean paradigm
As a lighted curtain following gravitationally down
Into the sonorously lit happening or descriptive
high
Left ordering about the state of play
Who left wandering about like a highland sea note
Life with a natural high- kind devote
For a summer input innuendo
Shadow arose like glory
Set back at the distance
O'er the frothy wispy undercurrent
The sunny bliss, a sullen memo stands
Where as a dance falling understands

In flail of radiant shafts lit beauty
Shall the glen ever be happy again.
There is an apple edifying in the blow
Rose red petal in the Autumn gloom

The divinity all gardeners and farmers grow
Sweep out the store yard openly blow
Like efficacious wheat germ in the mix throw
As in the original nectar to fall as snow
In the red-bricked pan-tiled warming waves
Effusing droplets fall sunlight sunlit evening
Wandering in the shafts across the meads
Where the slim youthful Canadian swan feeds
A mellowed Negroid cormorant swiftly swims
As clouds lift upon sun warmed mountain tops
Weary of each dispassionate breath
Watching the exhaust communication breath
Feeding the trapese gleams risin' sedge
All along upland mountain jelly beach edge

HALO'WES SON SARI OR I WALK

I walk through fields of clover
feel warming summer sun.
I walk 'neath Willows weeping,
Where sparkling waters run.
I walk across the hill-tops,
I see valleys down below,
Where waves roll o'er the green fields,
As soft winds gently blow,
I see bloodied poppies
(Ablaze in golden wheat)
I see the bright horizon
Where heaven meets
Across the Atlantic gulf stream
I see clearly beneath the beech trees,
Through bluebells, like a sea
Of never ending blueness.
Into eternity knowing
Tomorrows winds clearly calm.
I walk down lanes between hedgerows,
Where dog rose briars entwine,

And foxglove spears reach skywards
Through old man's bearded vine
I walk through orchards heavy,
With blossom on the bough,
I walk through verdant pastures
Untouched by man or plough.
Into the cobbled farmyard,
Where feathered fowl roam free
And gaggling geese bantering
Their welcome out to me
I walk through this ol' England
How long will it remain?
Will it be here tomorrow
When I walk this way again.

TORVISCON DAYBREAK

Its dawn breaking, the skies a hazy blue

The trees wake as the day begins to dawn

The birds chirp and energy so serene

As if in a mesospheric moist dream

Each passing breath breathing golden corn

Sweeping past ones face in breath of an
embrace

Timorous peck of lore and form

Of beauty expressing emotions instruction to
please

Calming voyages high on the aerodynamics

Albedo radiance of breath over a mountain
waking

When all is a beautiful day ready to its waking

Where a breath of might has all been a pleasure

Ready for day to breathe, as a breath of a rising
bull

or a cow absorbs moisture ready for a day to
graze

As the morning lifts, in a crowing chirpy heat
haze

The sun peeps over the mountain in a radical
rainbow around its globe.

Rotand Pass / Rohtang Pass

A snow pass in the mountain ………

Up to the highest peak I know

Where skiddow's roam on the snow

Perfect slopes on which to ski

Yaks and furr, chi and onion omelette

The snow gives pride in its change of aspect

The slightly freezing air, ice squeezes out of gath….?

Come January it must freeze mo…..?

Very few animals gather here to stop

Though refreshing

Still the jackdaw with his yellow

From Natural Allies

Willows bend over the river's edge,

Sheltered too is the waving sedge.

The warbler sings upon the rush

And the sad dry wind blows with grace.

The ancient mill wheel once ran for years:

But now there's tourist crafts in done-up barns.

Hillocks with copses of Scots pine and chestnut

And the sunlit shades on gravel deposit

Up in the trees blowing high and free
Their shadows fall, like seeds of energy,
Fed by the light of the rising moon,
Along the banks of the Glaven in June
Melodies drift across meads so rhythmically
grown,
The hedges where the holly stands alone;
The rippling river meanders the marsh;
Peace instilled away from life so harsh

HMP CADIZ

Life is the high mountain in the stream,
That comes like a river and into my dream.
Looks like I can't see it now.
Seems like I can't hear
Cities drawing near.

Long in one mountain, high in the scream,
That comes like a river and into my dream.
Colours turning read
In the eyes of my head
As I wake and rise from my bed

CRUNCH

At the rise of the twisting of facts
Like an inhuman wish to falsify acts,
Within its means, a bunch of twisting dreams
And uncertain lies. The Crunch. Their pious
schemes
Falsify award with self-seeking
Using educational good will and notoriety.
Humanity! Like detritus feeding fish,
And children, simply believing a wish.

Material harmony, struggling to protect,
Like a language with a simple dialect
Passion, like a moist wind coming with a beautiful
scent
Of heather aroma, calms the mind.
So now we must invent
A way through of these complexities.

And you? With a new ego inflamed
Accelerating towards change
Rocking our brains.
New standards to our names,
Everybody complains.
It is lessening the bounty within our store
And we're put off by an impossible score.
I wish it were as before,
For us to rearrange later.
It's a hard climb to remain the same
And sometimes we are truly 'up against it',
Yet you have new images for us to fit.

A SHAFT OF LIGHT IN A DUSTY PLACE

The sun within the atomic element,
Through a glass pane it shines.
As if through a diamond it gleams:
Instilling warmth in the dusty atmospheric space–
A comfort on our faces while we absorb
Vitamin 'D'.
Into the water the sun does both,
Warming and glistening
Like a sparkling stream.
Gravity plays an integral part:
When the warm air rises
And frost its power prizes.
Opening rooted rocks from high pinnacles.

Time passes, we've One planet
To arrest the sun in positive ways;
This is a fact, it's how we react
Together we're open to its cause.
We must develop proper uses of its power
After all, we are touched by its light.
Everyone hopes children will grow up bright,
Individual too, with the roots of common sense.
When we wake up, all thoughts rush:
Birds chirping in the moist bush
Eating red berries and the like—
I'm off and away, composing on my bike!

RED SQUIRRELS

Listen here, if I were pulling the string
I'd change almost everything.
Rid the forests of the American Grey
Like the coypu it's been terror long enough
Yes, that'll be an end to that.

I'd like to see an end to horror and disease
See creatures happy and at ease
March hares o'er fields of muddy maize
The moonlight's clear, escaping clouds sparked
their craze.
Not so depressing, admiring willows bending
in the breeze

.

The native fox used to compliment
Red squirrel dealing with its nuts
Hurrying about like royalty with condiment.
Then there's the magpie whose character is
doubtful
He goes robbing nests, about in the wood

And he calls as if to make his strategy clear
They're used to the human element, precocious
in fear

And his peculiarity, He knows he'll never fit
But in hops of beauty, he absolves his despair.
So don't try to tell us 'it's all the same'

It's harder to keep your pecker up! It's a bleaker
game
It's rougher when you walk alone, down a
country lane.
That in nature's melding, all these creatures
politely syncopate
Lazily they pass summer days, til collecting
begins afore the wintry slumber.

The mind breathes with the organically
nutritious food to share
They all go about as if they still lived in a
medieval age
They're much more resourceful: they learn
each bit well
And only wish for peace here, and if you want
to know
Only at dawn does the Raven freely roam.

A cocky little bird strutting, swaggering as if to
say
He's the real magician, who'll sit upon a
headstone of sombre grey. sombre grey.

THE UNIVERSALITY OF TRUST

The cupboards of my mind are empty
I'm searching at a loss to find,
The energy itself to struggle along:
I might have used repetition too much
Fall from grace; be out of touch.
Black as the feelings;
Shady become the dealings
But from the frame-work; the competence
The logic, mind building brick;
Even when, I'm right at the end of my wick
I'll try and make the right times stick.
The cupboards of my mind; are full
So full are they I travel lightly blind
I'll try and speak from sense
I know not, where it came from whence
Waken up, and not be so dense:
The reasoning is part of the spirit
All the confrontation one can save,
I'll try and be more brave
Not give into the instance, I am on a wave!
I'll try and tally unto
And be generally true
For an everlasting vibe came through
Out there on the edge of space
The stars shone too;
And covered the Earth in dust
To filter the light that came through
In the universality of trust.

THE SEASON TO BE

I'm searching to be true,
Away from emptiness and depth.
Just struggling through:
Trying to find a key to turn to let me
through
'Cause there's very little else for me to
do.
Too materialistic, weighing me down:
Eating disorder,
Ambitious dreams, fractious beginnings;
Never grasping the energy all-abounding
Of the friends, these whims surrounding.
Time to flow, brief release from duty,
Welding in relief the beauty,
Trusting where the bonds seem supple;
Sights on a winning double
A rainbow arc for all the trouble.
Participation for the duration:
But no-one wants it at their door:
Unloading burdens, expectedly like trees
in autumn,
Thinning out the posing complexity,
Like painting with dexterity.
No knowing the whys and wherefores,
An abstract knowledge,
Within I'm searching to be true,
Up from the depths of emptiness.
A life to fulfil, an omnipresent will,
Defend one's ways

ALLEGORICAL AS THE DAYS.

The world is full of trickery
In search of the distance.
A little time to think sensibly
And breathe the breath of happiness.
To keep one's treasures nearby
However humble this humility;
Trying not to be discordant with virtue,
Or lost in the rigours of simplicity:
Regain once more the social cue
And wit enough to think for others.
The laughter she shines the view flowing
slow 'n' easy
Of these surrenders I knew.
When I was light in the mind just now
made easy.

SAD ENVIRONMENTALIST

I feel a little disenchanted

Like the protectors at the Gates of Hell;

A notion of stupidity and an idea of what's going
on

No strength in the muscles,

Too bewildered to break into what might have
been,

Too docile to jump from the fire,

Lethargically wrapped in futility;

Resigned, or designed, to drop

From God's equanimity,

The bottom room in the house of life.

How many times can we awake,

As we begin to slip passively

Further into the abyss?

How many chances must we waste

Before we join in the journey through the stars,

Between each galaxy, lifting up

Through the in-between and to sleep like brothers

In the knowledge of what we ought to have done,

Not what we ended up doing or might have been?

Then you think: If they think this about me and I
am.

In the effect the same as a child (the soul of which

Includes those starving in backward social situations)

My father must be sad also; and you slip into a

Psychosis of anguish your life, your intimate friend

Cease to inspire one's destiny.

You are ostracised from knowledge of yourself,

As those streaming past the Gates of Hell. Simply

Think... Simply think... You will not realise

You're devastated to the extent that your body is giving Up the Ghost:

Your mind sad with cares loaded against

Your understanding, and you have to adjust on such occasions

We are brought up to be peaceful

As a child of the Universe:

We tend to think of the Earth

With gut reaction:

Akin to that, we return to our mother (Mother Earth)

The milk of life on which we are weaned,

Adapting to our circumstance.

Do unto others as you would them unto you.

Continue along different openings: Open your eyes!

Lift them to morning light on a fragrant pasture.

Feel inspired, with senses tingling,

In the pleasure of happy experience

And a bright awakening on a new plane.

DUSK TO DAWN

From out of the mist comes the nightjars'
churring call,
Within, like a mystique, swooping to and fro,
out from where the trees stand tall,
Over the meadows to where the watery air's
slow to warm
The woody oaks along the edge,
Or to the establishing of it's precincts, away
from the North Winds.
As she begins her flight to feed the owlets all;
In the quiet farmyard grain store, the mice; a
flutter stills their struggle.
An anodyne to obvious aid, comes in colours
of stony black
In lesser forms the rooks call, which wield,
they happily thread
The sensitive flight-feathers that give to flap
Where their Autumn lands are still suited to a
Ladies Smock.
Throughout sunlit spells, the ravens will strut
to and fro, their raucous call,
Or like a climax species, a rook for stony flints
to seek a haven
The wisdom of which is coy; and for your
attention's a raving.
Similarly the mountain ash will colonise a
gentle scree or sheltered corrie,
Enough shelter for the lowland birch, a
blackbird comes along.
For the blackbirds everywhere can dwell, in

hamlets
or just a kirk,
As long as every day food does abound
throughout the year.
But where the birds on salt-marsh flats, their
warm-blooded sense
Sends us wondering from where; and how they
come and hence
Their mating plumage shows a more
spectacular scene,
for nature in its balance is such a wonderful
theme
Which keeps our dreams down a rivulet,
rushing over shallow reefs.
The shell-drake on crustaceans feed, poking
about upon the shelly shore.
The nearby copse of trees and meandering
breeze
And all is once again the nightjars' hunting
ground,
A tonal measure, searching in the melancholia,
way beyond,
Which we with adjustments to, and not against,
The beautiful harmony around,
That we in our existence mayn't feel so very
much alone,
The dawn of nature's harmonious peace.

TIME TO TURN THE TIDE

Time to turn the tide and rejuvenate oceans
worldwide
Arrived in a maelstrom of cider and fun
But returns seven thirty, up early to run
down to the holy town for a tune up and busk
Hoping quite quietly for a blade of tusk,
Sort the chafe out from the husk,
Equality unity is only a small ask,
A balanced approach to a neighbourly task.
Up early with cheeses and coffee, not in a
flask.
Venus shone and The Plough and the great
Orion
Distance check, calendula eye bright and
byroni
The first morning is cool and bright
And slumbers refreshed all through the night,
A world to greet the friends of light,
An impression to last holding on fast,
An approach of shared stories and fate,
Time to turn the tide if it's coming,
Before it's too late

STAYING SINGLE

Do I love her?
Deep down?
Are we gonna meet,
Now I am in town?
Just an hour.
Sight seeing,
Our love renewing,
Or am I dreaming
Of sweetness and change?
Shooting stars they rearrange,
Sending stardust onto our brains,
In our hair a tingle,
And she appears, from out of the crowd,
Where with guitar playing,
Did mingle – just single.

INTERSTELLA

If I could explain
I've tried to display
The brighter side of my day.
I really have genuine good Karma.
The time I've spent professing good intention,
Supplemented by the odd good invention,
Which is a contribution to a solution
Needed at any expense, life will assert
Bring needed moisture, Mother Nature to
convert,
Life to breath in grace to impart
Our visions captured naturally by our heart,
Rounding a curve of time torn struggling,
Emphasis on assisting people's life juggling.
Try to embrace an honest tract,
Our empathy and solace largely in tact,
Verging on sympathies, one singularity packed,
Upon a journey, a path carefully edging along,
Putting ones foot when its standing and strong,
Like a crystal structure honed and out,
Painstakingly looking for highlights to surface
in the prism,
Cooling in a wind of perspiration and love,
Knowing oneself problems to rise above.

CAMEO

As I sit within a wall painted room
Trial images from out of my mind loom;
The level of thought precariously thin
I paint, in candlelight atmospherically dim.

White cracked plaster, became a blue sky,
Concentrating clouds as they sail by;
Loving high, branches intertwine
Rows of trees along the headland dine.

Waving in the sky, over a wading road
Man is wading, sun in his heart
The brown sludgy weed-stream depths
An imaginary destiny collects.

Distinctive yellows now will yield
A wind-swept sun-drenched corn-field
A secret belt of dark distant rain
Some humour to help refrain.

Inquisitive pheasants, arbitrary game
In amongst hedges, poppy flame:
Sight somewhere has been pleasantly kind
Plastered all over the room to unwind.

CONSEQUENCES

Open on a melting block of ice in a pool of water.
It drains off and alters a balance.
A big stone ball is set in motion.
It helters down a chute, and skelters off the end.
It knocks over a tall edifice and a pack of white rats are
tipped out.
They run on to a surface that is part of a large trap.
The trap is sprung.
The displaced air causes a wall to fall.
This tips a balanced container of water.
The water streams towards three glass poles with lit
candles on top.
The water rocks the poles.
They wobble.
They rock.
They crash to the ground.
One candle sets alight the ground which is covered in
petrol.
In turn this ignites a fuse.
The fuse burns along and up toward a high cross
member.
When the fuse reaches it a sword will drop.
Underneath is a beautiful baby.

Get real.
Live green.

Stephen cook and Alan Fleming

ECLIPSE OF VIEW

Tolerance goes hand in hand with freedom
flagellation is the vibe even
within the astute idea
projected from
outward
in rhythms
with beat of time
in accordant paths of lime
a hardy quick to reach climax
should a lime
continue as
a species
of lime
as a
tree
upward
Into the forest
of sensitive calm thin
whiffs of puff or just stuff
a wiffs of trodden rough turf
lead to stubble, speedwells and calamine
accelerate thought visual or rare
is the love gradually to share
lowly upon chancing upon a meadow lark song
when time in the hourglass's near you
its sands tinkle
in slow jets or plumes of his love.

LATER WHEN I WOKE TO TAKE TEA

I saw it majestically restructuring its walls,
I answered it's energy but others followed.
Growing o'erpowering, penetration calls.
Till all I had seen was swallowed.

Later when I woke to take tea,
I remembered in a heat of perspiration
How happy life was meant to be.
And I sat back to control the ovation.

Perseverance towards stable olfactory
Is normally captured in notes diversive
importance
Like an unwanted set of improprieties
Left to dangle aimlessly at the mode

In controlled changes of the mean end
Knowing the conditions are largely self.

LENNYS FARM

His cows had wrecks for friends in their field;
Warm paddock pastures, set aside:
Short Thorn Road: The scrapyard branch;
Silver Farrn for a car or a bike to ride.
You may have heard of dudes on a ranch?
Well, Lenny's was run along this line.
A Ford Transit, and it went just fine.

The things a smooth handler,
Bottom line was 'bought as seen', when sold:
Price adjusted with getting under way;
A slave battery, for starting from cold
As you pressed the pedal, engine revving
His sense of humour was seldom ebbing:

The life of a chassis was predictable:
A wing would unbolt, or engine parts swap:
Ford pilots, Austin found a stable:
The Medlar family had opened shop.

I'd been sorely tempted one last deal to clinch
The Lancia Beta Convertible, lifted out by
Fordson winch,
Much sought after, technologically advanced,
for days gone by:
One of the Marques left twisted along the
edges of a muddy ride.

PENNIES FROM HEAVEN

A lady's role is sometimes lost in desire to exist

As the signals of destiny torque and twist.

This isn't too good:

Of Bodicia I recall she did battle,

To protect the walls and tend the cattle

Help forge an existence

And always trying to help man not to loose his mettle.

Not to loose his!

In such simple tasks I'd like to imagine, like boiling a kettle.

The rest of problems of strife

Come from finding time to relax;

In relaxing might need a few props,

A bit of sculpture, coloured door stops,

Some to steady one's hand in accomplishing a few ops,

Maybe even bringing in some hemp crops.

"Hey, slender beauty!" as her hand rends the oiled door.

THE GLAVEN

Willows bend over the river's edge,
Sheltered too is the waving sedge.
The warbler sings upon the rush
And the sad dry wind blows wi' grace.
The ancient millwheel once ran for years:
But now there's tourist crafts in done-up barns.
Hillocks wi' copses of Scots pine and chestnut
And the sunlit shades on gravel deposit
Up in the trees, blowing high and free
Their shadows fall, like seeds of energy,
Fed by the light of the rising moon,
Along the banks of the Glaven in June.
Melodies drift across meads so rhythmically
grown,
The hedges where the holly stands alone;
The rippling river meanders the marsh;
Peace instilled away from life so harsh

STRANGLING

Then a black limo with half-a-dozen came
And in whispers, in circle, of cigarette flame,
I think a little vodka was shared
My wishes my dreams; alive intact,
Witnessing the group, tugs arrive to the act:
I cannot be jovial be like a prince;
Fix their smile and their confidence con-vince.

They must know I've seen life inside out
There's nothing to celebrate now! it's not their
shout!
I know only a few bits and pieces; I know
where I'm about
I think that's respected though I feel a bit of a
lout.
Each person has position from which they can
give
To others show a better side of oneself - for
this all can live.
This is solely a mental picture known of
oneself
Which attainable close and presentable
With uttering a word nor displacing their
action.

I spent a winter in Turkey, on the road
Steadily thinner; that's releasing the load

Slowly the warmth fills in my heart to beat
As I once again pull over the Poly sheet
Into my dreams and slumber
Not carrying on much weight to lumber
I've smoked my very last cigarette
Tomorrow' 11 be a struggle on that You can
bet.

TABATHA

The farm yard's steeped in fascinations door
There's Tabatha the motley-coloured cat,
sheep, chickens, cows galore.
Where's this parting shot taking us, the people?
Want to know; The glancing riverlets flow.
The willows on the lea, bending sallow and
Ash,
Curtains draped on window sash, distant banks
lined with hash
And carpets come from Morocco.
Seas of wheat, belts of trees, wind-break early-
morning breaks.
All generally in good taste even the art a little
bit.

There's lumber to log, marsh orchids meadow
and bog
Posts to dig, fences to erect, property to
protect.
Individual dialect, sites and sights
Leave the fore-man on his round to inspect
Antihistamine lotions, potions for illnesses
under a vet,
tables to read, judgements for economy to
speed.
Advantages, disadvantages; liberally for labour
heed
Satisfaction and knowledge

THE SONNET

Here, today in my window,
I see a new face.
Life in the vastness of eternal space
Motley Clouds
Pass on their way
And meet the mystery of dawning grace.

If in eager conscience, t'was a picture of You
Justices tide rise up, lonely vapours adieu.
In a crucible the changing time
A signal to Autumn's wilting lime,
Our hearts burn gently, under loves mantle too.

THUNDERBIRD

A tramlined, white-lined, slightly-banked road
Motorcycle with twin hub brake and two-up load
A Thunderbird, heading out towards the sea-shore
wake;

Waiting for the stones and pebbles to roll
Amble over the phosphorescent sands, feeling free
Surf that falls in time endlessly
Our love, our freedom to extol.

Then into the atmospheric light
Hot air rising in an opalescent sight
Gliding though cosmic space
Weaving round corners, at a pace.

The easy note of a twin's symphonic thunder
Beneath the rail-lines; the road winds under.
Warmth and feeling of each other's human grace,
Riders silhouetted 'gainst the sky
Telegraph poles, shimmering trees, pass quickly
by.

On the beach, walked hand in reach
Their moments of union fleeting.
Onto stand in iridescence steaming gleaming
alone
In the morning shone a dark jet stone.

WALKING IN THE WIND

The wind beckons one out onto the track:
Nature walking, I'm going back.
Those oaks waving, with budding fingers:
Don't wait for passion no longer to linger:
Work now complete, a sobering heart-beat,
Soon the moon will rise over young wheat.

I'm out for an hour, just before dark:
The dog's coming along, we're out for a lark,
She's really cute a real furry doggy.
We're across the way. I hope it's na' boggy.
The meadow's sweetly fresh with freedom to
express:
I'm roaming the dales in warm winter gales.

Holly bounces along among a leaves swirl:
The road runs by the panorama to unfurl:
Browny red roofs, the beat of horses hooves:
Cares lost together, as our tale roves:
View flocks of sheep, near a sea of wheat:
And the moon is obscured by a dark'ning sheet.

TEMPERATE FOREST

The wind herald the changes of the seasons:
Leaves that give life to the supporting branch,
Vying with moisture brought up from the root,
The stains lends colour, as seasons advance,
Turns golden in the autumn wind.

But during the summer the wind is free:
Free as the breath from over the sea:
The changing moods, in which life surmounts
The logical mountain of somnolent events
Within the vitality of the seasonal spectrum
That forms the awakening of laudable nature.

Youth is born with a magic of creation,
Where, in a secret garden the curious may
enter,
Protected from the wind, growth of exotic fruit
to see.
Where tree nymphs whisper plaintive songs
Of an idyllic Heaven.
Surely in this place, where only gentle hearts
may go,
there are only laws of nature, unsolicited
Because this knowledge of one and all, like a
myth,
Brought down through the ages, to freshen
thought;
Shadowed by the evening, it's keys are the
dawn.

THE DHOW

To wander through the jetsam of years
unhappy people gaze upon us with tears
Pieces rise to the surface for us to pick …
Is there areal solution for the mind to be quick?

Confusion runs though cultures alike.
Riding resourcefully on a peaceful bike
Through war and devastation, where living
survived
The Dhow: A king of ships, whose journeys
thrived.

SUPPRESSION

Ideals are left to roam
Where I have no heart;
They cannot find a home
My Initiative to start.

No talent left to carry.
Or friend to laugh or joke.
No girl with whom to tarry.
Desires burn and choke.

The colour loses it's edge,
Naiveté is lost with increase;
Each field is cordoned by a hedge
And feelings lose release.

TRANQUILLITY

For all those that do despair
Join in the countryside care,
A gentle breath of fresh air
Can really be quite pleasing:
Chirpy birds that sing.

Come away from stress impure:
Relax in this curious pleasures
Which comes with no measure.
Fulfilment to one who waits:
So sit now and contemplate.

In some warm rays of the sun
A Day's course has just begun:
So float upon a cushion
View the perfect world of nature.

SELF ESTEEM

Further than the limits of my mind
The wit of memory being kind:
Further than my will to fight
Peaceful shining of its light:
Beyond cordiality on which I bend
The Sanctity found within a friend:
Beyond the lightening of a new surprise
Over a river, an impression of the eyes:
Further than the flood of bewild'ring desire
Is time, waiting for inspiration's fire.
My banished ego so lamely falls
Dying a death, where rhythm stalls
Beside the warmth of my mind's eye:
Inside fascination's subtlety.
The kind of world we leave behind:
A clear reflection of the space we find.
In what frame are we to build?
An ancient reign forces through a guild.
History's patterns, a display of judgement:
Where is the light in the thoughts it sent?
Newton's inventions: How far the thread?
Whose mouths shall feed upon a crust of bread?
Sharing principles, good for one and all.
Jokes only the knowledgeable can understand,
Pondering carefully, coffee in hand
If in the future we can live more placidly,
Re-learned interdependent harmony:
Tidal power, solar panels, economic cars,
Family planning, curb on extravagant desire,
Water mills turn, crafts and sensible technology,

For a positive reality, awareness of geography;
Future chances, organic farming, return of fallow:

Of the leads, which do we have lime to follow?
Love and peace, like an example to last:
Joy at a time, when troubles are past.

THE INTREPID SPIRIT

Where is the wandering eventually to find,
With heart searching free of bonds,
The graced moment unique and unblind,
A person can fulfil a purpose in life,
When one is constrained by fears
The guiding thought is sustained,
The gravity of the situation contained;
Only just enough is sufficient
And anything less is a burden.
Heed taken before consequences too dire;
The pioneer finds originality in skill:
The action is thoughtful,
When climbing that hill.

A COUNTRY ROGUE

There are two basic categories of emotion:
One is akin to physical devotion and
culminates in
highest form,
The other is mire of an understand flowing
from the heart
And results in love of knowledge's flowering
art.

The wayfarer tends his ills to cure,
He'll share his life with emotions pure
But his actions are seen in a flickering fire.

Oblivious are his natural sites,
Like a stranger walking through mercy camps,
Lonely and thirsty, there footsteps he wearily
tramps,
A loaf of bread to buy, or just postage stamps.

And now too thirsty a dry throat says,
Too far down unchartered ways,
More than just an oversight this World to heed.

Too rhythmical this pen of fear
Too Empty each syllable written there,
Worked on, braided empty and shelved,
Too deep the mind has delved.

SUPER TRAMP

The axe which a with man may reap a better
field
Is the greater evolution of cares subtle yield
Turning faster, spinning out into space,
Affecting men's hearts with bonds of grace.

Come out from poison of an ungrateful streak:
Learn to express words, once unable to speak,
Taking the brunt of man's feud with the
economy,
Being caught in whirlpool of regretful sodomy.

Attracted by a gimmick, an easy-speak,
Gummed up inside, exposed, tired and weak,
Damned from the outset – Cocooned in life's
intrigue,
Completely out of one's depth in a different
league.

Balancing on a treadmill, fatefully kissed:
Unable to capture anything inside, shaking in a
mist,
Breathing like an alien blindly searching truth
Taking all sorts of anything a nourishing broth.

Out of sorts, shunned in man's will to out-
shine,
Youthful energy come quickly to the loss you
find.
For all those feeding dimly with their palms
Take them into your heart with open arms.

GRAINS OF SAND

To gaze upon the sunlight of creation
And watch the tides ebb and flow;
To hear the thunder of the falling wave,
Unleashing latent wind-power and moon's
frequencies;
The silver passages of light dancing on ripples,
Strong in the temptation of knowledge's
abundance ...
And the futility with which it can be washed
upon the shore.

Here is a place where the weary can unwind:
The therapy of an endless roll of breaking surf.
Happy, sunny summer days, swimming and
sailing,
Fishing with nets for shrimps, which tickle the
toes,
like an annoying sister, in playful mood of
love,
And piracy! Washing away many an intricate
sandcastle,
Built lovingly with bucket and spade in an
artful medium.

This restful play of children along the golden
sands,
Hiding among the marram grass, which
anchors the dunes;
To perceive the desert in awesome loneliness,

and think
Oneself lost in some romantic place;
To walk in salty zest to a quaint café:
The warmth of an inspired atmosphere,
Absorbed by life near the sea an a sense of
well-being.

NIGHT-JAR

How can I take to the wing?
How can my spirit fuse within
The twilight of the evening?
I wander at dusk feeling wise.

Floating about in freedom's limit,
Where expression is just benefit:
Agreements measure, searching in a fire.
Night comes slow and fuses with desire.

NATIVITY PRAYER

Come and wake a seed two thousand years
sown,
Germinate this seed two thousand years grown.
I know poets write your story,
I know painters paint your glory:
Immanuel birth
For all on earth,
Our friend understand
So stem your hand.
Blind by invention streets
So starts, Peter completes.
Guide by thy love's abundant source
For peaceful harmony born this Christmas,
Christmas 1980.

WIND

Trumpet shimmers of damp meads
Across to new life sprinkled fragrance force;
To salt marshes where the greylag feeds;
The winged air of suspended intercourse,
Migrants of a Capricorn sky come flank upon
flank
Descend to ruffle the surface by a water bank,
Human ventures increase, sails
reappear,}Benevolent nature Bemused in a
summer's fare
Instil deep impressions, willed in sun's bleat;
A canopy to infinite cares that love has cast,
Confident and open with secure heart,
Theses breezes spur with sportsman's art.
The ceaseless cares of this season's gift
Makes the mind beam into visions shift;
An unmade bed in autumn's carpet,
Richly vested into cascading light, let
Through the shameless branches cracking
To and fro o'er the still golden bracken.
On a cold winter's night an echo tracks its way
Through dawns evolution of sorrowful grey,
Weary tears stream down a winter hardened
face,
Lightning forks cross crystal door to open
space;
Contemplative of directions of the mind
The memory lives, far reaching, long behind.

BUCK
(Ex Greyhound Racer)

The proudest animal, I'd chance to have,
He loved it down on golden strand:
With pure joy, real freedom far and wide
Over blowing sand in a bounding glide.

His beautiful head swaying, tongue out one
side,
He'd be gone like a streak …
If only they'd speak …
So friendly, so full of loving …
His good nature made you weak.

MEETING MRS LOCKE
by Trevor Nocknolds

Meeting Mrs Locke
Knitting worlds with her fingers,
I forget that I forgot
Where my girlhood lingers.

First thing in the morning
When I wake my cup of tea
I watch it from my window, crawling
I hate the slinky sea.

It took away my Billy
It took away my husband
And I know I'm old and silly
But I know it wants my son.

I watch his boat out crabbing
(See-sawing on the sea)
I would cast my hand and grab him
And bring him home to me.

WORKING HARD

My eyes feel gummed
Like two ice-cold toes numbed
In a wet rubber boot.
Shamed and drugged.
This heart there's nowhere for
Just a barren plain
Or chipping footholds in outcrop mountain
Called insane.

I'm purely absent-minded
Because I'm slightly disorganized
I need help in this area
And pray where I'll be.
But looking ahead
Peace will probably preside
And I'm sure we'll cure disease
And all our axles grease.

NOT TOO TOGETHER

I just feel the signals
Are liaisoned with the weather
Even when you're not too together.
Is this why I am so down?

Just a job but I feel like a clown.
I just want to scramble my thought
Come out with the bits which fit
Like a photo-album I'd flit;
Til the Autumn Maple leaf
Peaceful squit, ol squit!

Someone can make sense of it
A little singing tit;
Bluebird – the ingot
Of colour in the mind
Keeps us company
When friends find

As long we help somebody
When we are able
Like all these guiding stars
When the ship is unstable
Reaching for home
Now we can sit in peace and quiet alone.

THE WEAVER'S WHEEL

Let us continue with our life's play
Even protect our light of day
I wish to travel
Unravel
Be able
And stable
Reliable
Even if understated.
Peace in our time – we have waited
Our doctrine we have stated
Destined to wear a thorn
Others kneel and pray
While uttering words which they quietly say
"In peaceful meditation
Within the surrounds we pass the day".
Happiness is all abound
Growing up from the ground
All as in nature, we have found
A welcome hand to tend the land
And set a path to meander for a while
Alternative directions, a country style.
Along the violet clad meadow wild
And shapely cottages pantiled
Curved and angular, among some trees
Scots Pine lifted by the breeze
Amber and vintage-green ferns sparkle
Ancient oaks of fantastic shapes
Sunny South-facing hillsides with grape
The heron steadily took off and flew
In the mind and see the folk far below.

WISHING

The peace within stays steady
The place and within is ready.
Within is mystical and magical
The state of being, in the palm
Resting upon the knee
In a state of energy.

An aura surrounds the soul
And has seen us reach our goal.
The mechanics of living hold a key
Upholding each others' destiny.
Struggling to sustain a happy life:
The energy to face daily strife.

Within calm surrounds the mind
And all troubles float off behind.
So sometimes people catch you unaware,
Then all your thoughts are surely there
Making your smile one to know
With friendly radiance all aglow

SYSTEMS

It was amiss to be so nervous
Say something or take the ride,
Or drop a clanger, still the flow
Jump the gun, or simply overrun.
On these occasions, it's good to have
Someone to know —
So there is love on which to rely
And all my troubles say goodbye.
Humanity wishes for peace to arrive
A crusade of understanding needs to thrive.

Lily-of-the-valley with a sheaf
Like tiny baby milk-teeth,
A lion protecting a cub, a squirrel hoarding
nutty grub
Dancing in among the maple trees,
Which bud with an aroma
to set the mind at ease.
In nature's confidence and I feel nearer
The hub of nature's bounce
Selling love, by the ounce.

THE JACK RUSSELLS

I exercised a bit
And feeling fit
Went for a walk
With two Jack Russells
Named Plug and Tubby.

Here today, a new face
Mottled clouds cleared the place
Pass away on a sunny day
Where kids can play
I stroll off at quite a pace.

Striding up the road,
Releasing my heavy load
Troubles disappear
As does my fear when I'm feeling free
Upright in my mode.

I'm going to run to the moon,
I'm going to get there very soon
And sing me tune:
'Praise the Lord'
Thank you Summer sun.

Into the miasma of life
Searching amongst strife
Tubby's the mum, blind on the run,
Plugs's the offspring
Soon to have more.

Little puppies to adore
Springing round 'pon the floor
From them dolly moved the day
But better done by a stud
Better Plug living with better blood

Too deep these questions:
Would they be spotty,
Straight-haired or curly,
Or speckled and dotty
Dancing prettily in circles.

WANDER

In amongst the grassy dip
Down the vale in Winter's grip
Out across the plain
Knowing exercises gain.

Standing awhile to compose
Feeling the sun's warmth
Falling on the face shows
That Spring is on its way.

First, out to watch a tree being felled
Rope and a cut to gently fall
Its top is slowly is slowly brought down
'Till on the ground is its crown.

Ploughed fields all around
Loamy brown ground
Ready for planting if it wasn't so wet
And fields of corn to set.

Past the barn down the farm track,
Along to Kerries and back.
Two horses on the meadow
Easterly winds do blow

PROCRASTINATION

Havering – delay, put off
I wanna see you
Roll this joint
To the rhythm of the fire.

Friends and family
Being led by the Tzar
Loyalty split and our maidens wandering
Each little toke I'm savouring
And wondering how we are
Going to get out of here.

THE BED I LIE UPON

Bed is a place where I ponder
Bed is a place where I see yonder
Love is a project, a cunning scheme
How to win her on the scene?
Be polite, or hope to dream?

I see Norfolk floating in the sea
Crumbling faster than eternity.
Is it because of pesticides
Our butterflies are nearly extinct?
Or bees dropping off in honey-making?

Man will see his Rose drop pinker
And evolution is on the steady blinker.
Has poor Darwin lost the farming battle
Let alone world peace?
In the scrap-metal trade rail lines torn up,
Freight congestion, it's Manic indigestion.

Yet still I lie in my bed, slightly ill at ease
Though there's aspects which still please,
Like the study of pollution in French rivers
And altering the way we treat our hedges
Three metre strips and all that lark
Might be a passage of light through dark.

And we might see yonder
These are thoughts easier to ponder.
People ought to utilise gas in their cars
Space ought to be for admiring stars
Aeroplanes ought to pollute less
And carbon monoxide be less profuse.

But these kind of postures in bed!
Are sending crazy thoughts to the head
As man appears to be losing the thread.
Rain hasn't helped and, like an egg,
What we have now is just thoughts
About future weather.

SMOKING LAWS

Are the Dutch more at ease
With their smoking laws to please?
Hemp nitrofies the soil
And stores excess moisture
It would absorb carbon as it grows
As well as making fibre and Oil.

Life around Hempnall shows
It was once
Pleasant on the meadows.
Oil should not come in tankers
Filth for all this richness.
Aren't the ideas about hash al wrong
With care about chillums we'd grow strong.

Generations and happy nations
Should we go our own way?
The Dutch royalty have given
The people the right to say.
Dear to their heart, they are level-headed
When hash is the subject.

ON MY BEACH

Sitting here in the peace
With being steady
The senses all feel release
But I am ready to deal.

This is the English dilemma
Rushing to compose
A steady beat to say
The beauty of silver, of the rose.

I don't want to face
All the turmoil of the fantastic rat-race
So recently I sat on an Indian beach
All the girls to beseech

The waves to swim in and adore
A pretty and clean shore
All the rubbish within reach
Where the restaurants clear the beach

Ready for the men with the collecting truck
All the visitors wish them luck.
The cows still go up the streets
At a slow and steady pace.

Got to have a wealthy soul
Aiming for that love goal
Up to the Loekie Bar
To listen to unrehearsed sounds.

My return I just can't wait
Even a spell of punk hate
From Manchester musicians
Recently at the Edinburgh festival

It's a bit of an anti-climax
Better try and relax
Try and live reality
And don't forget hospitality.

It's a people dream
Fit healthy people on the scene
Out from the banyan on the road
Monkeys in trees , people out to please..

PROCREATION

Procreation – that's some belief
Baby born of creation
All that internal relation
Everyone a happy nation?

Into her name to be,
When it came to me
Wandering off quite slowly
In a joyful undertaking.

An assignation
A path to follow
Whether deep or shallow
The way is narrow.

Sure and Polite
Following the light
Sparklers in the night
A firework show.

Upstairs a radiant glow
Memories of someone I knew
A wish I sent from below
In land-sea blow.

Eating fish with friends
Then up to 'The Seahorse':
Happy dissipation

Here's all you need.
Hindu or Christian
Buddhist or Muslim
Vegetarian or fish
It doesn't matter what's on your dish.

We are all learning
We have somewhere to go
Many people to know
Either way the wind will blow.

As I'm drinking my caro
And then Masala tea
P'haps ginger, lemon-honey chai
A girl with her tits out

Makes you think!
And if she gives you a wink
I think I'll write
This down in ink.

I DID THIS PAINTING

You could paint this one in a room
With elegant allure, lines and curves.
Ask her if you're getting on her nerves
And ask her if she's warm and comfy.

Drape her with a blue sari
Hope all her curls pass,
But I'd like to add one curl
This baby to unfurl

Must look after her skin
She'll divine her instinct within
With a line to compose
Hand her a rose —

Or a Hindi flower
In gardening power
All active in her smile
I did this painting and it took a while.

You can wear a condom
The choice is yours
Is this hurting within?
A thought is lost, is this sin?

The answer is obviously 'No'
But then where does this go?
Intervene in another's code?
Into the distance I rode.

NIRVANA

Blown-out in frustration,
Procrastinating
On a journey of self-denial
Disintegrating car!

Pictures gone afar
Nobody calling on the phone
Like a bird losing it's voice
Singing totally alone

Begging for mercy
Like a hitch-hiker in the cold
Forgetting the theme
But feeling very bold.

DOWN BY THE STONE
(2014)

I had an anchovy
It tasted salty in brine
I paused to recover
But my father had explained to me
It would take some time.

So I thought about this for a while
I was nearly down by the stone
And you and I took a toke after a mile
Then I was no longer alone
And we were laughing in style.

RUSSIAN BLONDE

It came to me
I had gone afar
My wandering star
Oh! heh la la,
I am guided
Protected and provided
Waiting for Gold Flash
—A motor-cycle to ride
Upon the circuit.

I am ever hopeful
Of the prospects
Of efficacious fruit
Or a girl who's really cute
I pray I can connect
Or I'm waiting to.

Perhaps a little hash
Smoked in a chillum fine
A wish of squash
Cross the winning line
The game laws a sign
That we all play for the time
The code is the referee
Helping us until we are all counted free
Hemp products work like ecstasy
The word is happy to be.

All the rivers run free
With innows and trout
And the ditches are like the Dutch
We'll ask these servants of the State
Why Hemp Laws and hash has
For years been made to look rocky
Everyone drunk, obese and cocky
Will answer, "Because we like a drink"
But a blonde drummer, Katya
Smoking a pipe made me think.

Like the sun shines through the glass
And warms my face
There are so many stars
In the Russian sky
Not so many cars and a girl must pass hours
Like a wish the river Neva flows
Where it goes
Only the One will know
What is in my heart is
Better than the state.

FEAR OF GOD

When in dire straits
It's as if no-one waits,
But the trowel on concrete
Or the industrious heartbeat,
Sweltering sea of wheat –
Or a lorry wheel that squeaks and grates
Passing cars in spates.
It's fresh crabs and salad dishes
It's children not harmed in wishes.

Growing to observe beauty and admire
With the indignity of a country squire;
Gallantly in goodness never tire
But, in jealousy, there are bounds:
It's as if you walk on hallowed grounds.
But when you're acting like God
Bound by fear – there's no-one near.
We've to remember, God's a lonely old soul
And occasionally you need the feeling of a
good goal.

But variation keeps us cool
Understanding all sorts, never playing the fool
When only judgement can save
But, if you never swim, you're far from being
brave.

YER ALL IS OPEN WHEN YOU'RE BLUE

I sit her and wonder why
It is that I must sit here and cry
You might thinking this too,
You may understand the feeling blue.

Blue hat feelings are soon forgotten
Float way when you're feeling rotten
Carefree, under a banner
In such a complimentary manner

You read me a poem in Madonna blue
Now I'm writing, maybe falling in love with
you.
What's the point, when all is lost?
Our departure at such a cost.

Yer all is open when you're blue
And you're having to join the crew
But everyone must have a honey
Bees to the blossom maybe sunny.

THE NEARBY ROAD

Rubber and tarmac
Dominates my day
The car rules the roost
Laws about bicycles sway
Exploding traffic lights
Solar-pannelled roads.

Where's the human contact now?
Blood ain't flowing now, holy cow,
Just the odd roar or rumble
But tigers are nearly humble.
Children are young ephemerally
Old must dress in peace cleanly.

The passage of time has been relaxed
Learning about cities
All the tastes you can score
Libraries at your door
Technical colleges uni-s galore.

But it came to me for five
That it's hard to stay alive
Local services are weak
Strangers, so-to-speak;
Expeditions when you are tired
Going to bed, feeling wired.

Lack of human touch
Internal fire – nothing to say, really, very much?
Just a swish of cars goes on for hours,

People discuss their powers
About as much as the equations of life.
Stand firm and face the strife.

MO

I knew an aged Jack-Russell cross
Called Mo. She often barked
When she wanted to go home
But when she went for a walk,
She'd lark about upon the rocky lane.
There was no telling where she'd gone
But she'd be along in her own time.

Slowly wriggling in the summer sun,
She was friendly to cats,
(An unusual trait)
And for sausages she could wait,
Grumbling as she took the bait
After that, she'd settle, she'd had lunch.
When we were all happy, we'd have a smoke
Mo would be mumbling, oh she was such a
joke.

YELLOW DALLIANCE

I am sorry I was born
(I'll try not do it again)
I am the thorn.
Lemon zest for thought
Is very carefully bought.

I am very tense
More rhythmical I might make more sense
Yoga breath One to Three
Actions are massaging the tummy
The kids all say their first word, "yummy"
But I just want their mummy.

You and I had better act less dense
Sacred variants speaking with eloquence,
Yellow dalliance and purple compliment.
I'm not sure whether to stick my neck out
For a fancy bit on the side
I just want to ride
Or even better simply confide.

THE NUCLEAR DETERRENT

The Nuclear Deterrent promises pain,
Suicide and martyrdom:
To the front, with no one left to live or die for.
Teach, preach or understand, as you are inanely
led
To a point of agony,
Which is supposedly pertinent
To the relevance of being on earth.

The Nuclear Deterrent, however
Is a scientific conundrum
Which only those who've stood
Within the doors of War
Could know the score.
For this dance 'on fire'
Is the chance to learning
About the reverse side
Albeit a confrontational proton
Able to render unto mankind
It's data message of reason (with the seasons0.

The Earth is a resource
Of which there may be another
Out in space – the race, however
Is to sustain peace, refrain from War
Live by as a gentle, fun loving creed (as one
can)
Spoken as the Word, created in the beginning.

For the colourisation, in a peaceful way,
Of an otherwise empty universe,
As lonely as the tormented souls
Under the threat of nuclear deterrent.

The understanding of Christ's
Tolerance of pain is the beginning
Of reason within the astute idea
And life is the struggle to perpetuate
Being in harmony and considerate
Both to neighbour and animal
Because he made his cause clear
For both man and woman.

A solar jet, hair net, fishing net or a safe bet?
Is like a fairly intelligent Morris Traveller With
a devious allowance for the sake of inventor.
Then of efficiency? For a universal world
system...
Worth its weight in gold?
If only ...
Bought or sold to persist
With right from wrong;
We could be free from nuclear deterrent
Which is an awfully big bomb.
Brings only

Hysteria and loss of civilisations simmering
crust.

The seconds are ticking
For society's fabric fashion of life
The seconds are ticking, for trouble and strife
Recording of carbon age
There's a kind of package
Of inter-relation
Shifting its goal-posts
From time to time
Succumbed to injustice
Of mere predicament
And sold in stories
Films and parodies.

AROMATHERAPY

In a massage parlour I began with a girl
gracefully.
She seemed so polite and surprisingly faithful
She came in effort, strong, soft or gentle
As she soothed away sensitive tenseness I felt
her mettle.
There was nothing heavy coming up above
She gradually manipulates and
Then she tried a little reiki
To see if she could like me
In moments she filled me aromatically good
Hallucinating mysterious pleasure working till
then understood
My night before was dark pulling clematis tree
Taking it down to the farm incinerator, it smelt
pleasantly
The fire of love within me burns.

WILL & MOTIF

It's always how to feel
Or the Guest for comfort to deal
The Nursey allies could make this become real
Our habit cannabis to unseal
Possessions real
Voice politely chuckle
Odd snippets to unbuckle
Real in a life to compose
Reflects the pulse they expose
With a wee little hustle
We can survive the hastle hassle
Sometimes we feel we're in a bit of a fussle
We're aware of differential people
Rearrange to a perspective
Remembered in a box collective

THE MARSHAM MEAD WE DUTH

I love to rest, unaccompanied by stranger
feeling
I get great pleasure, where it comes within,
A gentle circulation in the morning sun,
Away from the rushing traffic each day begun,
Crackle of the frying pan of mushroom
omelette enjoy
A plan for the day, each task then deploy
Like learning to mark time, just with a sister
Threading a chain of chain
Learning menstruation, emotions slowly fuse,
Sometimes in friendship, we later fear to lose.
The value of nature – each fright forthcoming
Albeit the sight of fluffy red squirrel running
A falcon hovering over our meadowland as
well
Or the sacred memory, a flock of geese
swirling who have fun
Floating up in the air in great display
Animals appreciation of our efforts their was
Seem a given for to recall as harmonious
Some picturesque blessing on a sunny day.

WEE TOWN OF KINTYRE
(2018)

It's dawn now, the wind is blowing strong.
We're on a beautiful planet, where we belong.
Hearts are open to the pressures of the weather.
We tend to strive for one direction,
One where we can see clearly when we're
together,
Striving for another century our protection.
We're his children, the passage is thru,
It's exactly up to us, just thing we are the crew.
Wake up early, with sunrise and morning dew,
Lights of Cambletown Harbour sheltering
The many ships which choose a day in port.
After all it's pleasant people to the town have
brought.
Wake up to the white froth of the harbour
entrance,
Where we took a small craft to retrieve lobster
and mackerel,
A wee puppy called called Bosin on the bow,
Anchoring up in the lea and raising the tackle,
Crabs snapping about in the well
Mackerel on the line, three or four.
A healthy meal we can have, a good deal,
Salad , tomatoes, lettuce, carrot and cheese.
The fresh air from the breeze
All day, makes us happy and easy
On the bed to rest ans sleep away

KNOTTY WALNUT

Like a tree planted by a forbearer
Once dreaming of a place where it blows
Or cleaning out the covers, to the river flows
Where the kestrel swoop to catch lunch
And Lightning reaches down to sever a branch.

That hung and shaded festering airless,
Beneath the clearing created by the Ash
For now a small veg patch created in a flash:

Where the garden wall freed from damp
And the girlfriend walked serenely with a lamp
The rainbow of light glowing in every red brick
Will warm in the midst of the morning sun;
The gender is released in the day to come.

THE LONDON TOWN
INTIMIDATION

I walk brusquely into the old town
Not thinking of anyone in particular.
I glance up, look around,
Watch aching arms, flick the switch.
The light 'blows'.
What a time to go.
Ah! The Bitch.

If you were a female low-grader I'd be OK, but
I'm just a fired, touchy soul
Who has been working live a slave since the break of
day.

Do you still have happy memories up from the mine,
Covered in soot, sending up the goods
To keep houses warm?
The hearty Welshman's sings
As he walks home from the mine.
I long for freedom,
Just like anyone, alone on this globe.

Still, I don't like the categorisation.
Be articulate, try to break the ice.
To be unintelligently nasty isn't very nice.

Am I allowed to learn about my world,
Without prejudice and 'Sizing up', for arguments sake?
Not looking 'daggers', calculating and cold,
Are people allowed to make you feel awkward, lost
and prematurely old?

KINSHIP OF CHANGE

I traced the earthly initiatives
At roughly a quarter-to-six upon a windy night,
Kids all coming home for tea,
Some already there watching TV,
Experiencing life's universiality.

A vista of English countryside,
A green area far and wide.
Friends are off to the Phoenix Festival
Trucking about the marvellous meadowland.

One is learning about everything, everyone, all
alone.
The lie of the land, the interfaces
And boulders lain in time far gone.
Organic eco-spheres emanating messages of
settlements.
Held within the clasp, in his grasp
A simple understanding handed down a trust.
The knowledge, intricacies and perspectives
Within breakdown of space and its dust.
Watching the river flow,
The majesty in mountains lava all aglow,
Reducing in ashes in its wake,
The lasting changes in the shadowed surface
make.

BLACK SHADOWS

A two-laned, white-lined snake.
A motorcycle with a twin-hub brake.
Heading out towards the sea-shore wake,
Waiting for the stones and pebbles to roll.
Amble over the sands feeling free.
Surf which falls in time endlessly
Our love, our freedom to extol.

Then into the atmospheric light,
Dark, star-lit spangles night.
Gliding through the cosmic space,
Weaving through the corners at a pace,;
The east notes of the twins symphonic thunder.
Beneath the rail-lines the road winds under
Feeling the warmth of each others' human
grace.

Shadows from the moon, silhouettes against
the sky
Telegraph poles shimmering trees pass by
quickly
That on the beach they walked hands in reach;
The moments were fleeting, their hearts are
beating
Till onto the rest the machine in streaming
The polished chrome is elegantly gleaming
They walk to their houses under the steely
wisps of
miasmic light.

SPACIN' OUT

Daughter of the oncoming dream
Wave of energy, yet to measure
Cloud of a youthful stream
Fall upon my frailness with pleasure.

Distance of yet uncharted globe,
Hope of an instance, still far away.
Come upon the naked idea, with a robe.
Make easy the gift of love I pray.

Truthfulness be my gift to offer,
Memories be good and not fade away.
Contact to express that inner feeling there
Some other time, upon a future sunny day.

BLACK – WHY BIRDSONG

In my short life, useful though it may be
With people who adapt I find affinity.
The children joust with spirits of craziness,
Long faces, cheesy smiles,
Tongue in cheek, so to speak,
In the lamp of life's filament.

Best work when the situation requires.
The meaning of what is free,
one learns successfully,
Can easily dissipated be.

If one's co-ordinated unrelated,
Reluctantly, I'd like to make alterations,
Walk in the vista of life's contemplations,
Through banning of opulent slothfulness.
Working it out with greater composure,
Just a touch of innocent carelessness,
Can avert over-reacting incompetence,
To find a line of pure common sense.

AZTEC IN A CHANGING WORLD

Touching closer to the margin,
Area of enchanted thought:
Tempering a daily task,
Ponder in a drift
Thinking which shift
Subtleties queue, wearing the mask.

Gaze at the moon
In clean starlit air.
Listen to the rhythm on shore
Joy in acknowledging dreams
Collecting torques and shells
The mind in greencap dwells.

A happy land, all in one flow
Adapting slowly to changing signs
Alive ecologically
To cure and protect
The land and life with thought select.

EPHEMERAL

Disturbed as in a mist frightened by lightning
An awesome phenomenon of ecospheric harmony
Or like fungi assist the organic goodness
Rather than the crow flies,
That break our wonder and surprise

Wish to open eyes, shake off this phoney disguise,
Break our knowledge time and again, so our roots
grow deep
Our vision in the hands of grace, watch o'er our
sleep.
The vistas are seen, with time to absorb
Our food is plentiful and pleasantly stored.

These moments of the season, when we belong
The moments of summer, times of strong
Incidentals; like a fluffy cloud that hovers
Purposely aloft, in time and space;
Forming imaginary patters, before our mind,
Helping to break with the hum-drum, role of the
day
Gainfully light-hearted and happy today.

SOMEONE

Well you've gotta protect your soul
Stretch out when the white light
Warms your body ecstatically
In the host of some vibey friend
Who lay'n near
Always finds your ammunition,
Pinched muscles, that flutter and flee away.

Wondering though age old stories,
The memory warms, in the day
And your body like a river flow.
Yet this meditation, is to know.

Protect your mind in rhythms:
Of lovers, sumptuous wave of arms
Unsubstantial mind, cleared in experience
Of the reality; in the alter ego;

Change too vast, moves too fast
And one is drawn to truth
Where, you wish to spend a while
What we'll be and who and when to know.

LOVE

She the pains you disdain
Like a weather vane
Protected from insane
Love to the same
Niggled with stain
Come again and again

Cajole and adore
Your mating song
She sure belongs
Smoothing rash feelings
Like a copper beech
Yearly copper-bronze thoughts reach

Momentous in a war's history
Are all directions in check
Because people look over
The invaders they swish and fleck
Like a hound with insistence, name black.

When the only image of yourself is OK
It's the one you project.
Chance and luck ironies fountain
The significance of life
These possessions to protect

One must be a person of sincerities corner
Sworn her, sitting no more than little Jack
Horner
Loves devotion trying to step across
A memorable covert bridge.

The power of light has warnings
Ladies smock, water-cress all over
The red sky at night, is a mantle
Of love's currency
And may your message seek still waters
For a little bird to calm ribble of daughters
swishing.

A wondrous adjustment to the world by
everyone
Like tidal love, communicated in invisible ink
Within wisdom's safety cover, people turn to
joy
The will of a workman's art, is practical alloy.

ART WITHIN THE CRYSTAL

Don't spread oneself so quickly
Spread oneself too thick
Find friends to be troubleless;
Spend time on oneself;
'Godliness is next to cleanliness'

Drop no dangers with nearest or dearest
Life is free,
Life is easily defensible;
Learning everything of the intricacies of time,
In the breakdown of space.

But in practice, the climax
Generation of your own garden,
Is happily abundant,
With happiness extras, such as;
Coal its, Blue tits, Sparrows, Plovers and
Partridges.

SHALLOW ASPIRATIONS

These reflections
Character inspections
In the way, your human vein;
Ghost of a reason's mode,
The scorning anode and cathode
Every creature awakening:

Depending
Ascending
Into terrestrial space
Intending
Impulse spreading
Beauty and purposely
Appearance of that medium, *Life*

Little aspirations
Come unfounded
Like an empty pit of luck,
Or limited freedom
In a kingdom:
The mark of the individual
Mildly confused

Example misused;
The aim exploited
And human reason
Become hollow
With no love to follow

If one has an accessible imagination
Which can be both funny
And is reassuring you
Mellow reality of the mind.
In communicating inward feelings

Which need a vent for normality
i.e. One's status quo
One's initiatives
One's libido
One's Assessment on intention
For any successful amenable catharis.

TRINKALD

When I'm feeling OK,
I am a scribe
To instil the sights outside;
The sounds around to imbibe
Sometimes or often I can scribble;
Thoughts trinkelate
When I take trouble
Future feelings percolate
Pictures of beauty I can take inside
like a God to inscribe
But I just feel tribble
Like a dry river ribble
Through towns and villages, past the rabble
Toward the sea, in a wandering watery gabble
Over all the rabble
Reality pops up, as if a babble
Like a fish with no bones
A sponge needs to reinflate
Hassles float off, like a floating raft
Upon a submergence of water
with nothing in it
Bare - gain

Vane, insane, no pain
Lame;
The messengers are bereft
Anyone with any confidence has left
To hide like a seagull in a croft
A cliff eaten into by the wind.

Whose why change
Rearrange
Evolutionarily finned
Earth just grinned
And formed a face on the cliff
A new cadence, a rift trying to find peace
within the storm
Upon the morn.

PUFFING

It moves the mind
Into the picture entwined
Meaningfully thoughts filter through
By the sinful snow-white moving along
whose freedom melts upon the eyelid
And nothing but feeling warm as a kid.

Nearby there's a rivulet starting out to the sea
Enervating air stirs surface around the lee
And on the beach coarse of the shore
Come the fishermen with Tilly lamps
Casting out for fish galore.

The transcending curtain of evenings
A pure image of greater space
Wildness tamed, in hamlets asleep
Self lighted windows and smoky stacks
Roofs with snow falling on their backs
And the Moon's sugary paleness buffing
The memory of a slow-train puffing.

PROACTIVE BIRDSONG

In my short life, useful though it may be
With people who adapt I find infinity.
The children joust with sprits of craziness,
Long faces, cheesy smiles,
Tongue in cheek, so to speak,
In the lamp of life's filament.

Best work when the situation requires.
The meaning of what is free
One learns successfully,
Can easily dissipated be.

If one's coordination is unrelated,
Reluctantly, I'd like to make alterations,
Walk in the vista of life's contemplations.
Though bashful of opulent slothfulness
Washing it out with greater composure.
Just a touch of innocent carelessness,
Can avert the awkward exposure.
Thus avoid over-reacting incompetence,
To find a line of pure common sense.

STEADY TEMPERATE ISLE

No Need for sprays moistening summer days
Justice for the trees.
Justice for the bats and bees.
Justice for the biennial seasonal change.
Justice for the rivers.
Justice for the otters
who make our native banks.
Tell me Great Creator
Please make us a plan.

We will begin variation
interplant beetroot, wheat, barley and potatoes
Following hedgey moisture-kept panorama
induced-picture
Nodule rope-making hemp
Release moisture for albedo droplets-filled sky
Sun-diffusing at harvest
The old plant decomposing beneath.
Deeper the field of lime and brick earth breakdown
Has all the nutrient,
The flocculation of elements
Find a niche with silky soapy air bubbles
That allow the roots, as one has thirty yards
Each side of hedges to stop the wind
Blowing away the moisture to hold
In times of drought.
And creatures of nature fly about

THOMAS BROWNE
T. P. 21

CAMBLETOWN HARBOUR IMPRESSION
Steve Cook ES9

Printed in Great Britain
by Amazon

23133551R00076